WHAT'S UP WITH WATER?

WHERE DO WE GET WATER?

by Karen Latchana Kenney

Consultant: Marla Conn, Reading Specialist, Read-Ability

BEARPORT PUBLISHING

Minneapolis, Minnesota

Teaching Tips

Before Reading

- Look at the cover of the book. Discuss the picture and the title.
- Ask readers to brainstorm a list of what they already know about how we get the water we use. What can they expect to see in this book?
- Go on a picture walk, looking through the pictures to discuss vocabulary and make predictions about the text.

During Reading

- Read for purpose. Encourage readers to think about how people get water and its role in life on Earth.
- Ask readers to look for the details of the story. What is happening during different times with the water?
- If readers encounter an unknown word, ask them to look at the sounds in the word. Then, ask them to look at the rest of the page. Are there any clues to help them understand?

After Reading

- Encourage readers to pick a buddy and reread the book together.
- Ask readers to name three things from this book that happen between when rain falls and when water comes to the tap. Go back and find the pages that tell about these things.
- Ask readers to write and draw a picture of something that they learned about where we get water.

Credits:
Cover, © Mike Pellinni/Shutterstock; 3, © Alex Staroseltsev/Shutterstock; 4, © Isselee/Dreamstime; 5, © Yevhenii Podshyvalov/iStock; 6-7, © Iakov Kalinin/Shutterstock; 8, © Shin Okamoto/Shutterstock; 9, © vovan/Shutterstock; 10, © robert_s/Shutterstock; 11, © kaninw/Shutterstock; 12, © Yuri Samsonov/Shutterstock; 13, © imantsu/iStock; 15, © J-Roman/iStock; 16, © LorenzoPatoia/iStock; 17, © CK Foto/Shutterstock; 19, © deepblue4you/iStock; 20, © Khosro/Shutterstock; 21, © CK Foto/Shutterstock; 22, © Studio_G/Shutterstock, © Macrovector/Shutterstock, © ptashka/Shutterstock, © Melodist/Shutterstock, © Pixel Embargo/Shutterstock, © DifferR/Shutterstock, © Weenee/Shutterstock; 23BL, © Mariusz Szczygiel/Shutterstock; 23BM, © kaninw/Shutterstock; 23BR, © ghornephoto/Getty Images; 23TL, © vagart/Shutterstock; 23TM, © varuna/Shutterstock; 23TR, © Schira/Shutterstock

Library of Congress Cataloging-in-Publication Data

Names: Kenney, Karen Latchana, author.
Title: Where do we get water? / by Karen Latchana Kenney.
Description: Bearcub books edition. | Minneapolis, Minnesota : Bearport
Publishing Company, [2021] | Series: What's up with water? | Includes
bibliographical references and index.
Identifiers: LCCN 2020039093 (print) | LCCN 2020039094 (ebook) | ISBN
9781647474935 (library binding) | ISBN 9781647474980 (paperback) | ISBN
9781647475031 (ebook)
Subjects: LCSH: Water-supply—Juvenile literature.
Classification: LCC TD348 .K46 2021 (print) | LCC TD348 (ebook) | DDC
333.91—dc23
LC record available at https://lccn.loc.gov/2020039093
LC ebook record available at https://lccn.loc.gov/2020039094

For more information, write to Bearport Publishing, 5357 Penn Avenue South, Minneapolis, MN 55419.

Printed in the United States of America.

Contents

Water When You Need It 4

Cleaning Water 22

Glossary 23

Index 24

Read More 24

Learn More Online. 24

About the Author 24

Water When You Need It

The puppy needs some water.

Just turn on the tap.

Water fills up the dog bowl.

But where does this water come from?

5

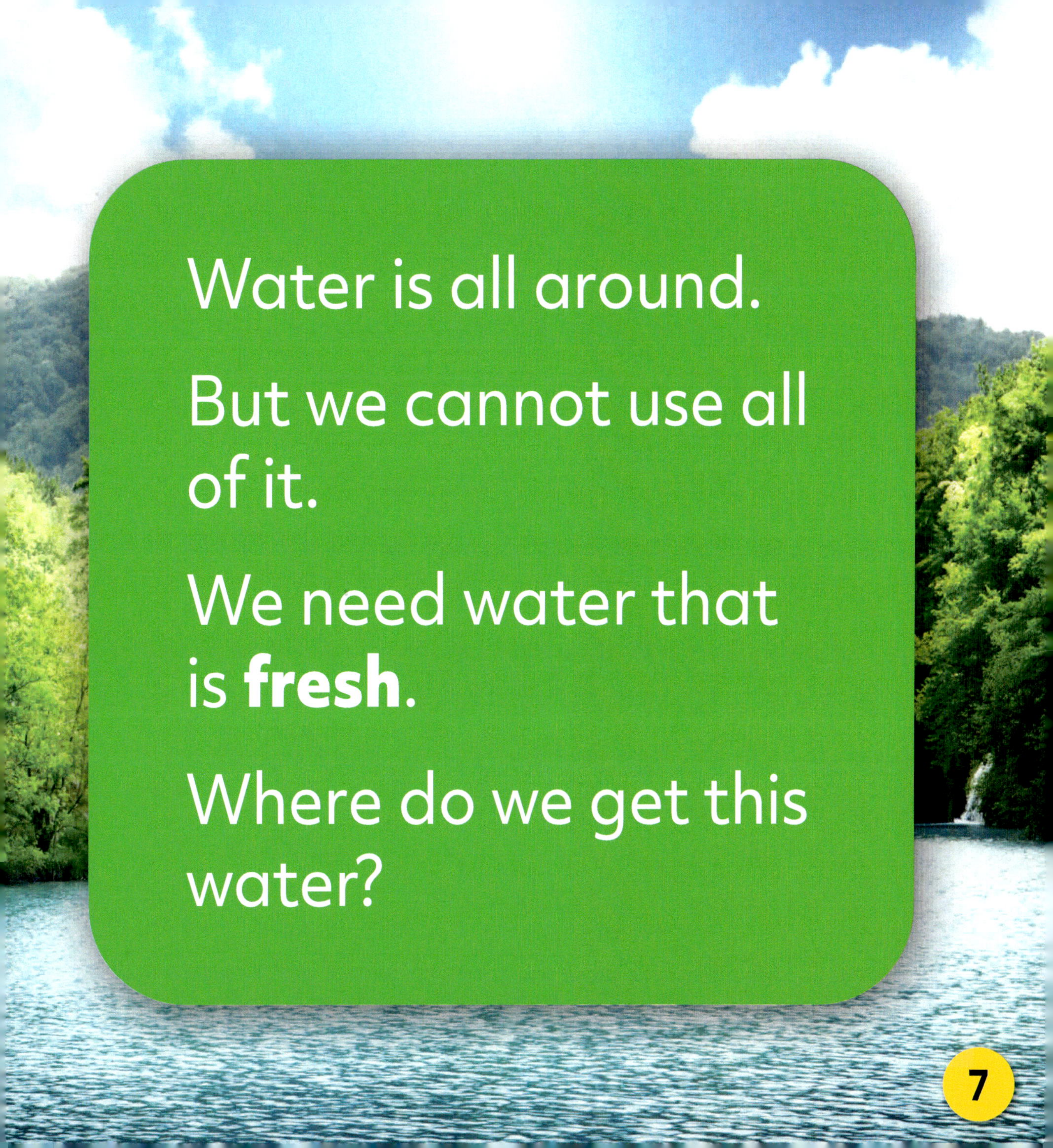

Water is all around.

But we cannot use all of it.

We need water that is **fresh**.

Where do we get this water?

Splash!

Rain is a kind of fresh water.

It fills up lakes and rivers.

Some rain goes deep into the ground.

Pumps take water
from the ground.

They take water from
lakes and rivers.

Where does it go now?

A pump

Water goes to a place where it is cleaned.

This place is called a **plant**.

There, they take dirt out of water.

They take **germs** out, too.

Pipes move the clean water to big **tanks**.

The tanks hold it.

How do we get that water?

A tank

We turn on our taps!

Water moves from the tanks to our taps through pipes.

We can fill the dog bowl.

Then what?

After we use water, it goes down the **drain**.

Pipes take the water back to a plant.

A drain

The water is cleaned again.

Then we have more water to use and drink.

Water comes a long way before it gets to our taps!

Cleaning Water

Follow water to your tap!

Glossary

drain a pipe that carries water to another place

fresh water that is not salty

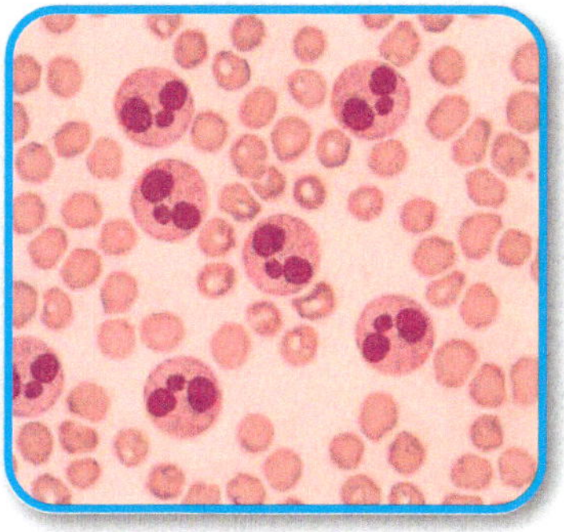

germs tiny living things that can make people sick

plant a place that makes water safe for people to drink and use

pumps machines that move water from one place to another

tanks large containers that can hold things, such as water

Index

dirt 12
drain 18–19
germs 12
pipes 14, 17–18, 22
plant 12, 18, 22
pump 10, 22
tank 14, 17, 22
tap 4, 17, 21–22

Read More

Chancellor, Deborah. *Turn Off the Tap! (Good to Be Green).* New York: Crabtree Publishing, 2020.

Kenney, Karen Latchana. *Why Do We Need Water? (What's up with Water?).* Minneapolis: Bearport, 2021.

Learn More Online

1. Go to **www.factsurfer.com**
2. Enter "**Get Water**" into the search box.
3. Click on the cover of this book to see a list of websites.

About the Author

Karen Latchana Kenney writes and edits books about water, nature, and famous scientists. She lives in Minnesota with her husband and son.